BIG FEELINGS

FEELING LONELY

by Mary Lindeen

NORWOOD HOUSE PRESS

DEAR CAREGIVER, The *Beginning to Read* Big Feelings books support children's social and emotional learning (SEL). SEL has been proven to promote not only the development of self-awareness, responsibility, and positive relationships but also academic achievement.

Current research reveals that the part of the brain that manages emotion is directly connected to the part of the brain that is used in cognitive tasks such as problem solving, logic, reasoning, and critical thinking—all of which are at the heart of learning.

SEL is also directly linked to what are referred to as 21st Century Skills: collaboration, communication, creativity, and critical thinking. The books included in this SEL series offer an early start to help children build the competencies they need for success in school and life.

In each of these books, young children will learn how to recognize, name, and manage their own feelings while learning that everyone shares the same emotions. This helps them develop social competencies that will benefit them in their relationships with others, which in turn contributes to their success in school. As they read, children will also practice early reading skills by reading sight words and content vocabulary.

The reinforcements in the back of each book will help you determine how well your child understands the concepts in the book, provide different ideas for your child to practice fluency, and suggest books and websites for additional reading.

The most important part of the reading experience with these books—and all others—is for your child to have fun and enjoy reading and learning!

Sincerely,

Mary Lindeen

Mary Lindeen, Author

Norwood House Press

For more information about Norwood House Press please visit our website at www.norwoodhousepress.com or call 866-565-2900. © 2022 Norwood House Press. Beginning-to-Read™ is a trademark of Norwood House Press.

Editor: Judy Kentor Schmauss   **Designer**: Sara Radka

Photo Credits: Getty Images: aldomurillo, 3, FatCamera, cover, 1, 29, fizkes, 11, 18, Hakase_, 11, JGI/Jamie Grill, 25, Juanmonino, 5, kate_sept2004, 6, Maica, 22, MoMo Productions, 21, SDI Productions, 10, 13, 14, 26, Thanasis Zovoilis, 10, triloks, 10, Wavebreakmedia, 17; Shutterstock: Teerawat Anothaistaporn, 9

Library of Congress Cataloging-in-Publication Data

Names: Lindeen, Mary, author.

Title: Feeling lonely / Mary Lindeen.

Description: Chicago : Norwood House Press, 2022. | Series: Beginning-to-read | Audience: Grades K-1 | Summary: "What does it mean to feel lonely? Readers will learn how to recognize and manage that feeling in themselves, and how to respond to others who feel that way. An early social and emotional book that includes reading activities and a word list"— Provided by publisher.

Identifiers: LCCN 2021026416 (print) | LCCN 2021026417 (ebook) | ISBN 9781684508181 (hardcover) | ISBN 9781684046706 (paperback) | ISBN 9781684046782 (epub)

Subjects: LCSH: Loneliness—Juvenile literature. | Social isolation—Juvenile fiction. | Friendship—Juvenile fiction.

Classification: LCC BF575.L7 L56 2022 (print) | LCC BF575.L7 (ebook) | DDC 155.9/2—dc23

LC record available at https://lccn.loc.gov/2021026416

LC ebook record available at https://lccn.loc.gov/2021026417

Library ISBN: 978-1-68450-818-1   Paperback ISBN: 978-1-68404-670-6

PO339N—082021

Manufactured in the United States of America in North Mankato, Minnesota.

Have you ever felt alone and sad?

Being alone and sad is one way to describe feeling lonely.

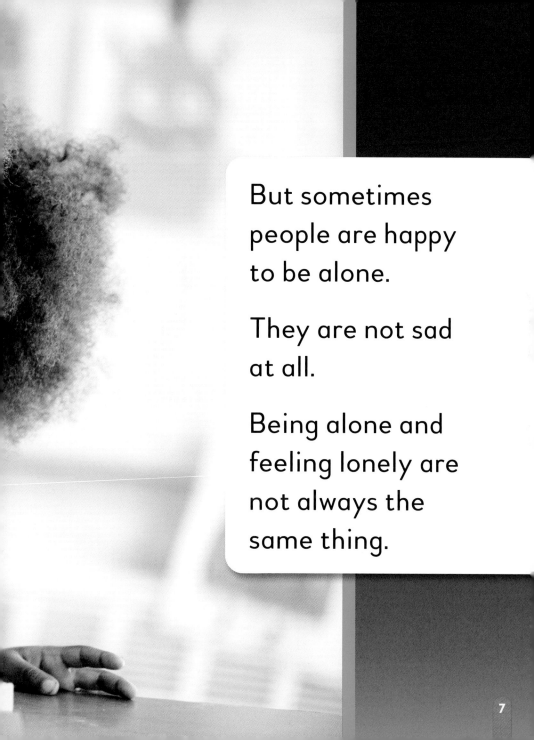

But sometimes people are happy to be alone.

They are not sad at all.

Being alone and feeling lonely are not always the same thing.

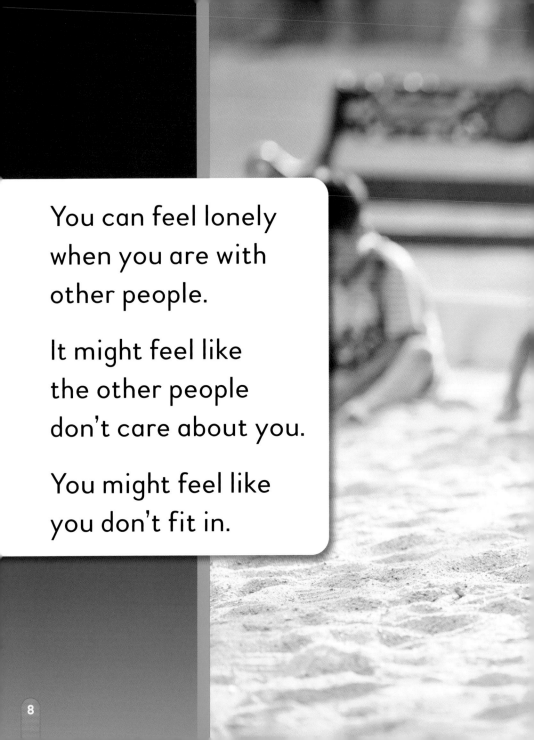

You can feel lonely when you are with other people.

It might feel like the other people don't care about you.

You might feel like you don't fit in.

It's not fun to feel lonely.

But it's okay to feel that way sometimes.

Everyone feels lonely sometimes.

Moving to a new school or neighborhood can make you feel lonely.

You might feel lonely when someone you love goes away.

You might feel lonely if someone is unkind to you.

It can help to talk to someone you trust about how you're feeling.

It can help to think about something else.

Read a book or go outside.

Sing, dance, or draw.

Do whatever makes you feel better.

A person who is feeling lonely might look sad.

They might be very quiet or act angry.

Everyone shows their feelings in different ways.

You can ask someone who's feeling lonely to join you and your friends.

Or you can ask if you can do an activity with them.

You might have a lot of fun together!

. . . READING REINFORCEMENT. . .

CONNECTING CONCEPTS

CLOSE READING OF NONFICTION TEXT

Close reading helps children comprehend text. It includes reading a text, discussing it with others, and answering questions about it. Use these questions to discuss this book with your child:

1. What does it mean to feel lonely?
2. What is the difference between feeling lonely and being alone?

Once you have discussed the above questions, ask your child to either draw a picture of someone who is feeling lonely or choose one of the children pictured in the book. Then ask the following questions about the child in the drawing or the photo:

1. How can you tell this person might be feeling lonely?
2. What might be one reason this person is feeling lonely?
3. How would you feel in that situation?
4. Do you ever feel lonely? When?
5. When you feel lonely, what do you do? How could someone else help you when you're feeling lonely?

VOCABULARY AND LANGUAGE SKILLS

As you read the book with your child, make sure he or she understands the vocabulary used. Point to key words and talk about what they mean. Encourage children to sound out new words or to read the familiar words around an unfamiliar word for help reading new words.

FLUENCY

Help your child practice fluency by using one or more of the following activities:

1. Reread the book to your child at least two times while he or she uses a finger to track each word as it is read.

2. Read a line of the book, then reread it as your child reads along with you.

3. Ask your child to go back through the book and read the words he or she knows.

4. Have your child practice reading the book several times to improve accuracy, rate, and expression.

FURTHER READING FOR KIDS

Allen, Brandon. *The Very Lonely Boy.* Herndon, VA: Mascot Books, 2020.

Corchin, DJ. *I Feel...Lonely.* Chicago, IL: PhazelFOZ Co., 2017.

Holmes, Kristy. *Feeling Lonely.* San Diego, CA: Kidhaven Publishing, 2018.

FURTHER READING FOR TEACHERS/CAREGIVERS

Mental Health America: Is Your Child Lonely? (For Parents)
https://mhanational.org/your-child-lonely-parents

MentalHelp.net: Loneliness in Young Children
https://www.mentalhelp.net/child-development/loneliness-in-young-children/

Understood: What to Do When Your Grade-Schooler Is Lonely
https://www.understood.org/en/friends-feelings/managing-feelings/loneliness-sadness-isolation
how-to-help-your-grade-schooler-with-loneliness

Word List

Feeling Lonely uses the 97 words listed below. *High-frequency* words are those words that are used mos
often in the English language. They are sometimes referred to as sight words because children need to lear
to recognize them automatically when they read. *Content* words are any words specific to a particula
topic. Regular practice reading these words will enhance your child's ability to read with greater fluenc
and comprehension.

HIGH-FREQUENCY WORDS

a	do	not	them
about	go(es)	of	they
all	have	one	thing
always	help	or	think
an	how	other	to
and	if	people	together
are	in	read	very
ask	is	same	way(s)
at	it	school	when
away	like	show(s)	who
be	look	something	with
but	make(s)	that	you
can	might	the	your
different	new	their	

CONTENT WORDS

act	draw	join	sing
activity	else	lonely	someone
alone	ever	lot	sometimes
angry	everyone	love	talk
being	feel(ing, ings, s)	moving	trust
better	felt	neighborhood	unkind
book	fit	okay	whatever
care	friends	outside	who's
dance	fun	person	you're
describe	happy	quiet	
don't	it's	sad	

About the Author

Mary Lindeen is a writer, editor, parent, and former elementary school teacher. She has written more than
100 books for children and edited many more. She specializes in early literacy instruction and books for young
readers, especially nonfiction.